RAILWAY
• HALSGROVE •
SERIES

THE WEST SOMERSET RAILWAY REVISITED

Don Bishop

Don Bishop

14/7/10

HALSGROVE

First published in Great Britain in 2010

British Library Cataloguing-in-Publication Data
A CIP record for this title is available from the British Library

ISBN 978 1 84114 918 9

HALSGROVE
Halsgrove House,
Ryelands Industrial Estate,
Bagley Road, Wellington, Somerset TA21 9PZ
Tel: 01823 653777   Fax: 01823 216796
email: sales@halsgrove.com

Part of the Halsgrove group of companies.
Information on all Halsgrove titles is available at: www.halsgrove.com

Printed and bound by Grafiche Flaminia, Italy

CONTENTS

MAP OF THE WSR

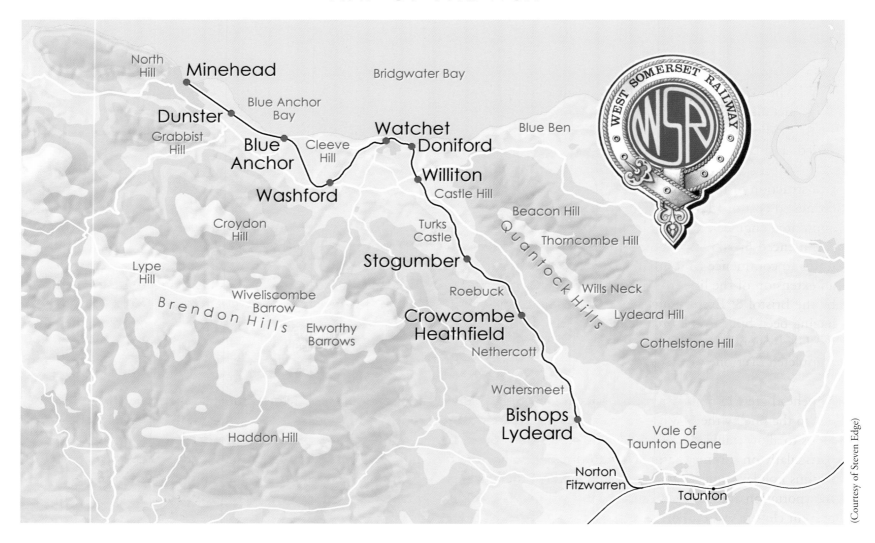

North Hill
Minehead
Bridgwater Bay
Blue Anchor Bay
Dunster
Watchet
Blue Ben
Grabbist Hill
Blue Anchor
Cleeve Hill
Doniford
Washford
Williton
Castle Hill
Beacon Hill
Croydon Hill
Thorncombe Hill
Turks Castle
Lype Hill
Stogumber
Wills Neck
Wiveliscombe Barrow
Roebuck
Lydeard Hill
Brendon Hills
Elworthy Barrows
Crowcombe Heathfield
Cothelstone Hill
Nethercott
Quantock Hills
Watersmeet
Bishops Lydeard
Vale of Taunton Deane
Haddon Hill
Norton Fitzwarren
Taunton

WEST SOMERSET RAILWAY
WSR

(Courtesy of Steven Edge)

INTRODUCTION

The West Somerset Railway is Britain's longest heritage railway, running for 23 miles from its junction with the mainline network at Norton Fitzwarren near Taunton, through rolling Somerset countryside and over some steep gradients to Minehead on the Bristol Channel coast. It is arguably one of the most scenic lines in the UK, with its very varied landscape from the Quantock Hills between Bishops Lydeard and Williton to the coast at Watchet and Blue Anchor.

Construction of the line was in two parts, the first section being from Norton Fitzwarren to Watchet, authorised in 1857 at an estimated cost of £120,000. The line was to be built to Brunel's broad (7ft¼") gauge, and indeed Brunel himself was appointed engineer, however by this time he was in poor health and died before completion of the line. Construction commenced in 1859 and after some financial difficulties which saw costs rise above £180,000 the line was completed for trains to commence running in March 1862. Subsequently another company, the Minehead Railway Co., was formed to build an extension of the line from Watchet to Minehead, which was completed in 1874 and the whole 25 mile route was worked by the Bristol & Exeter Railway Co. until that company was taken over by the Great Western Railway in 1876. The line having been built to the broad gauge presented some restrictions in early days in respect of through working to other parts of the UK by goods traffic. The directors of the line persuaded the GWR to convert the line to the standard gauge, work being completed over one weekend in 1882, some 10 years before the broad gauge's final demise.

Minehead grew in popularity as a seaside resort quite rapidly at the start of the twentieth century and improvements were carried out to the line by the GWR, who had taken over from the independent companies in 1922. These improvements involved extra loops to allow trains to cross and lengthening of platforms. By the 1950s "holidays by rail" boom, the line was always busy, particularly on summer Saturdays with through trains from the Midlands, North of England and London. The opening of the Butlins holiday camp at Minehead in 1962 kept the line busy, but with the increasing use of the motor car as a means of transportation and the publication of the infamous Beeching Report in 1963, the line was listed for closure. A campaign to prevent closure was initially successful, but doom and gloom prevailed as economies were made and the line fell into decay and a certain degree of dereliction. The much reduced service was finally withdrawn with effect from 2 January 1971.

Following this a campaign was launched to re-open the line under private ownership with the formation of both the West Somerset Railway Company and the West Somerset Railway Association (the volunteer support group) towards the eventual reopening of the first section between Minehead and Blue Anchor on 28 March 1976. The line was reopened in stages until being fully open to Bishops Lydeard in June 1979. Full restoration through to Taunton has remained a distant dream following firstly political difficulties involving the Unions and then the very high costs of rebuilding the line between Norton Fitzwarren and Taunton, following modernisation of the main line and signalling through the county town.

However in recent years the junction with the mainline at Norton Fitzwarren has been fully re-laid and re-signalled and trains are now able to run as regularly as required over the link. We have already seen regular Minehead to Bristol trains running and an increased number of through excursion trains over the link. Also the Network Rail High Output Ballast Changing Train runs frequently onto the line at Norton to discharge spent ballast onto the WSRA's land there and for use in connection with the construction of a new turning triangle. It is still possible that one day we may see regular passenger trains between Bishops Lydeard and Taunton and other destinations operated by mainline train operating companies.

The WSR has slowly developed into one of the country's leading preserved railways, now carrying well over 210,000 passengers per annum and indirectly contributing an estimated £6m to the local economy and employing around 30 full time staff and over 250 volunteers. The railway runs regular steam (and some diesel) services between Bishops Lydeard and Minehead between March and November each year plus a shorter period in December.

Today's West Somerset line starts at Bishops Lydeard Station, headquarters of the West Somerset Railway Association, with its museum displays and shop. The line immediately begins a 4 mile climb at a ruling gradient of 1 in 80 through some beautiful countryside to Crowcombe Heathfield, the summit of the line. There then follows a 6 mile descent through more fine Quantock scenery, passing the country halt at Stogumber, until Williton is reached, this being the halfway point on the journey and home of the Diesel & Electric Preservation Group's fleet. The line then continues on to meet the sea at Doniford before curving back inland at Watchet and climbing again to the village of Washford, today home of the Somerset & Dorset Railway Trust. A sharp descent at 1 in 65 down to the coast at Blue Anchor follows and then a run along the edge of the beach before the final 3 miles of mainly level track through Dunster and into Minehead, headquarters of the railway company and the location of the main loco sheds and workshops. In 2008 the railway commissioned a new turntable facility at Minehead and the area around the terminus was completely refurbished and now presents a much tidier and smarter appearance.

The line is base for a number of steam and diesel locomotives and rolling stock. It aims to capture the ambience of a busy GWR branch line and show some other historical features connected with the railways of the West Country in general. Its magnificently restored stations are a pleasure to visit and just sit and take in the atmosphere of a country station of times past. Much of this is due to the railway infrastructure all around, such as signals and signal boxes, lamp huts and various trolleys' etc, all things largely lost on the mainline network of today.

This book attempts to show the line in its full glory and show how it fits into the surrounding landscape so well. It is probably fair to say that the line is one of two halves – quiet countryside and bustling seaside. The undulating nature of the land around it, particularly on the "Quantock half", allows for some very scenic landscape photography to be achieved with the train as the focal point. I have tried herein to show a mix of scenic landscape-type views with some more traditional trains and railway pictures, and show some of the great variety of engines and trains that have worked over the line in recent years.

My photographic season is mostly between October and April, when the sun is lower in the sky and the light subsequently crisper. This allows the lower parts of the train to be highlighted and show up extra details, even from a medium distance viewpoint. During these months the cooler air also enables the exhaust of the steam locomotives to show up clearly and bring the picture to life, whilst in the warm air of summer it all but disappears, the only exception to this being in early morning or evening, and sometimes when near the coastal sections of the line. These months also mean that trains running in the late afternoon can be seen around sunset, producing some stunning "glint" effects – almost a holy grail for railway photographers!

Hopefully reading through the book will not only give you an idea of the variety of trains that can be seen running on the WSR but inspire you to visit the line, if you have not already, and perhaps try your hand at some photography in the wonderful countryside around it. If you do decide to try some photography yourself though, please do bear in mind that trespass on the railway's property is not only illegal but can be dangerous and should only be attempted when in possession of a lineside pass, available from the railway company at Minehead, and following some safety advice. Also please respect local landowners and do not trespass upon land without prior permission.

All of the pictures in this volume can be purchased as prints by contacting me through the website at www.donbishop.co.uk

Don Bishop,
West Huntspill,
2010.

A TRAIN FOR ALL SEASONS

We start the book with a shot of Prairie No. 5553 powering up the grade at Leigh Woods on 17 February 2008 with the 10.30 Minehead to Bishops Lydeard service. Very much a regular day-to-day scene in West Somerset in the early years of the twenty-first century!

Long-term WSR stalwart Pannier No. 6412 working a driver experience special past Bicknoller on 17 May 2005.

WSR-designed small Mogul No. 9351 climbing away from Bishops Lydeard at Watersmeet with a Minehead-bound service on 24 October 2006.

Opposite
The Bristol Channel and the Welsh coast form the backdrop to this shot of BR green large Prairie No. 4160 getting away from Williton with an afternoon train from Minehead on 27 March 2008.

Blue-liveried S&D 7F No. 88 approaching Leigh Woods Crossing with the 12.20 Minehead to Bishops Lydeard on 30 December 2008.

Pete Waterman's small BR-liveried Prairie No. 5553 working hard with a 6 coach Minehead to Bishops Lydeard train passing Bicknoller on 3 March 2007.

GW 38xx 2-8-0 No. 3850 passing Stones Wood with the 12.40 Bishops Lydeard to Minehead on 30 December 2008 with a specially laid on exhaust at this downhill location at the request of the photographer.

The lush greens of summer have arrived as No. 5553 heads the Quantock Belle dining train back towards Bishops Lydeard past Castle Hill, Williton on 18 May 2008.

BR Standard 4 tank No. 80136 running through Stones Wood with a Bishops Lydeard-bound service on 1 May 2006.

The WSR's class 117 DMU leaves Crowcombe on the final leg of its journey to Bishops Lydeard on 26 May 2007. The railway makes use of DMUs as a fill-in to the primary steam hauled services in peak periods and on some winter season services. At this time the unit was painted in BR green livery with small yellow warning panels.

Pete Waterman's small Prairie No. 5553 passing Turks Castle between Williton and Stogumber with a Bishops Lydeard-bound train on 1 May 2006. This loco has special meaning to the author as he chartered it to haul his wedding reception special on the WSR in June 2004.

West Somerset-based Pannier No. 6412 heading a Minehead to Bishops Lydeard service at Woolston on 3 March 2007. The engine was only able to handle WSR services in the off peak periods as trains had become too heavy for its modest power output and it was subsequently sold to the South Devon Railway in 2008.

Another aspect of WSR services is the vintage bus link provided between Dunster Station and the village and castle on bank holidays. Here a former Bristol bus passes along the main road into the village with the shuttle service on 24 October 2004.

The "Army DMU" as it became known heads away towards Blue Anchor across Kerr Moor on 24 August 2006. This unit in BR green livery with "whiskers" on the cab fronts was owned by the Territorial Army Transport Engineers for use in training exercises and loaned to the WSR for a period in the early 2000s. It has since left the railway.

GWR GOODS ENGINE TYPES

West Somerset-based GW 38xx 2-8-0 No. 3850 approaching Blue Anchor with a Bishops Lydeard-bound train on 22 October 2009. The engine carries a copper cap chimney which is not authentic for the class in GWR/BR days, although this is expected to be changed in the near future.

38xx 2-8-0 No. 3802 visited from the Llangollen Railway in spring 2008 and in glorious afternoon lighting is seen passing through Doniford Halt bound for Bishops Lydeard on 9 March 2008. The large 4000 gallon tender coupled to this engine was rare for the type as most were usually paired with a lower sided 3,500 gallon version.

The GWR also used the 2-8-0 wheel arrangement for a tank engine design for heavy goods traffic. Bodmin Railway-based Heavy Goods 2-8-0T No. 4247 is starting the climb of Washford Bank as it leaves Blue Anchor with a Bishops Lydeard-bound train on 17 March 2007.

The 2-8-0T locos were numbered in the 42xx and 52xx number series. A telephoto lens view of Pete Waterman's BR Black 52xx No. 5224 leaving Williton bound for Minehead on 9 March 2008. The engine has paid several visits to the WSR over the years.

Also in BR black is smaller GW 0-6-2T No. 6619 from the North Yorkshire Moors Railway which visited for the 2007 Autumn Gala and is pictured passing Bicknoller with 'Lydeard-bound train on 5 October 2007. This type was a development of earlier pre-grouping designs for use in the South Wales valleys on the extensive coal traffic.

In BR days a number of the 56xx & 66xx type were painted in lined green livery and the Swanage Railway-based owning group of No. 6695 have opted for this livery. An impressive exhaust in created by the tank at Liddymore near Williton on 22 March 2009 as it heads for Bishops Lydeard.

A shot which works well on a December morning with strong backlighting is at Combe Florey. On this occasion 38xx 2-8-0 No. 3850 works a Santa Special towards Crowcombe on 28 December 2006.

CASTLES AND KINGS

A complete contrast to the goods types in GWR motive power terms were the express passenger Castle and King class 4-6-0's. In this lovely "train in the landscape" scene Castle No. 5051 Earl Bathurst heads into the Quantock Hills at Nethercott on 17 March 2007.

During the engine's spring 2007 visit GWS Didcot's Castle No. 5051 Earl Bathurst carried alternative numbers and names for some trips and here makes a fine sight blasting its way up Washford Bank past Kentsford as No. 5054 Earl of Ducie on 18 March 2007. The engine was wearing BR green livery applied at the request of the photographer for the engine's final months in traffic before withdrawal for a heavy overhaul.

King No. 6024 King Edward I pays fairly regular visits to the WSR for galas and running repairs in between spells on the mainline network. On 18 March 2005 it run's along the cliff tops at Doniford towards Watchet with the Bristol Channel coastline as a backdrop.

The King passing Yarde Farm Bridge with a Minehead to Bishops Lydeard train on a cold but sunny 28 December 2008.

LORD NELSON

The GWR Kings were launched into traffic in 1927 as the most powerful 4-6-0s built, surpassing the Southern Railway's Lord Nelson Class. The National Railway Museum has in its collection Southern Lord Nelson 4-6-0 No. 850 Lord Nelson which returned to working order after a long and expensive overhaul in 2006 and did its initial running in on the WSR. Here Lord Nelson stands at Minehead awaiting the call to start running in trials on 24 August 2006. In the author's opinion the malachite green livery carried looks simply awful on such a large loco.

Southern 4-6-0 No. 850 Lord Nelson on a running-in trial working as pilot to BR Std Tank No. 80136 on a WSR service train passing Bicknoller on 9 September 2006.

ROYAL SCOT

The LMSR also had a powerful 4-6-0 passenger engine type and this too has recently visited the WSR. Royal Scot 4-6-0 No. 6100 Royal Scot, regarded by some as one of the most famous engines in the world, was restored to working order over several years under the auspices of owners Bressingham Steam Museum, Norfolk with the aid of a substantial Lottery grant. The overhaul however did not go to plan and a number of problems have come to light as work has progressed. The engine made its public debut on the WSR in March 2009, but not until after yet another problem hit the seemingly jinxed engine. A fire broke out on the lorry carrying No. 6100 to the WSR as it was passing Burnham-on-Sea on the M5 and its appearance at the Spring Gala was delayed as a result. With fire damage clearly visible on the front buffer beam No. 6100 Royal Scot is in steam at Bishops

Lydeard for the first time away from the works on 24 March 2009. The engine was not quite complete and was to make its debut as part of a running in schedule. Further problems have so far prevented the loco doing any further work at the time of writing in Nov 2009.

On 26 March 2009 the engine emerges from the small copse at Nethercott with the 15.05 Bishops Lydeard to Minehead, its first day in public service.

Opposite
In pleasant sunshine the LMS 4-6-0 No. 6100 Royal Scot passes Nornvis near Crowcombe with the 15.05 Bishops Lydeard to Minehead on 29 March 2009. The red livery is in fact incorrect as the engine is restored in its later BR rebuilt condition!

GALA EVENTS

At the other end of the scale in locomotive terms are the tiny Terrier 0-6-0Ts which worked mainly on the former Southern Railway lines. One gala visitor for autumn 2007 was No. 662 Martello and here it enters Blue Anchor Station with a three-coach local shuttle from Minehead on 5 October 2007.

Opposite
West Somerset gala events have become a must visit for many enthusiasts and are among the biggest events of their kind held each year. The spring 2009 event was based on a "Big Four" theme and the LMS was represented by Royal Scot and Black 5 4-6-0 No. 45231 Sherwood Forester, here passing Leigh Woods on 22 March with a Bishops Lydeard-bound train.

The Southern visitor for the event was Swanage Railway-based Bulleid West Country No. 34028 Eddystone, here passing Liddymore near Williton on 21 March 2009.

Opposite
The Eastern was represented by A4 Pacific No. 60019 Bittern, here leaving Watchet with a Minehead-bound train on 21 March 2009.

The WSR of course has its own fleet of ex-GWR locos but to help complete the theme at the 2009 Big Four event the railway hired in Hall No. 4936 Kinlet Hall. On 22 March 2009 afternoon walkers wave as the Hall puts in a sterling effort passing the site of Leigh Bridge loop.

For the autumn 2007 event LMS Stanier Mogul No. 42968 from the Severn Valley Railway attended and is seen working a late afternoon train to Minehead past Nethercott on 5 October 2007. Modern digital techniques have enabled me to alter the front four coaches to red/cream livery as a more appropriate match than the WSR's usual brown & cream for this BR black loco.

Against a dark showery sky Bodmin Railway-based Pannier No. 4612 works away from Doniford Halt towards Williton on 17 March 2005.

Quite possibly the ugliest engine to have worked on the WSR in recent years has been USA S160 2-8-0 No. 5197, here passing Leigh Crossing with a Minehead to Bishops Lydeard train on 2 October 2008. These impressively noisy engines were introduced to the UK for the Second World War and most were exported after the end of the war for service in Europe.

The rather more attractive lines of Llangollen-based GW 38xx 2-8-0 No. 3802 at Kentsford near Watchet with an afternoon Minehead-bound train on 5 October 2007.

Opposite
Steep Holm island stands prominent on the horizon as Prairie No. 5553 pilots Manor No. 7802 Bradley Manor on the climb of Washford Bank with a late afternoon gala service back to Bishops Lydeard on 10 March 2007.

Another recent eight-coupled visiting engine has been LNWR Super D 0-8-0 No. 49395. The National Railway Museum-owned loco was restored to working order and financed by Pete Waterman a few years ago. On 9 March 2008 the engine climbs past Water Lane near Stogumber with the Quantock Belle dining cars at the front of the train.

A further Midland visitor was Black 5 No. 45110 RAF Biggin Hill from the Severn Valley Railway. The weather for the spring 2008 gala was generally mainly dull and damp and those conditions persist to greet the Black 5 as it passes Leigh Bridge on 16 March 2008. The engine was in the last few months of its 10 year boiler ticket and being nursed along to take part in the 40th anniversary of the end of steam at its Severn Valley Railway home.

Another visiting Black 5 No. 45231 is seen with Bulleid No. 34046 Braunton in a pastoral scene as they pass Leigh Bridge on Sunday 29 March 2009 with an afternoon train from Minehead to Bishops Lydeard.

West Country No. 34046 Braunton made its gala debut at the autumn 2008 event and is shown passing Nethercott with a Bishops Lydeard - Minehead train on 2 October.

Opposite
Hall No. 4936 Kinlet Hall passing the intriguingly named Black Monkey Bridge on the climb from Blue Anchor to Washford with a Bishops Lydeard-bound train on 21 March 2009.

Recent tree clearance work opened up this view of the line at Nornvis Bridge just south of Crowcombe Heathfield. Swanage Railway-based 66xx tank No. 6695 heads downhill towards Bishops Lydeard on 29 March 2009.

DIESEL HYDRAULICS

The WSR also holds special events for enthusiasts of the older first generation diesels, in particular the Western Regions diesel Hydraulic types. In this shot maroon-liveried Warship D832 Onslaught and Western D1010 Western Campaigner leave Crowcombe Heathfield during the Mixed Traffic Gala on 16 June 2007. Note the "billycan" with a fresh brew of tea in its time honoured position in the cab window.

Warship D832 Onslaught running downhill at Leigh Woods with a late afternoon train from Bishops Lydeard to Minehead on 15 June 2007. The Warship is normally based at the East Lancashire Railway, but has been on long term loan to the WSR in recent years.

Mainline-registered Western D1015 Western Champion working a Bishops Lydeard to Minehead trip at Liddymore on 16 June 2007. The loco had arrived for the day on a railtour and was working this fill-in turn whilst on the line.

Another visiting Western, this time Western Loco Association-owned D1062 Western Courier, climbing past Leigh Bridge with a Bishops Lydeard bound train on the afternoon of 14 June 2009. This loco is normally based on the Severn Valley Railway.

Then DEPG Chairman Bob Tiller takes Hymek D7017 past Roebuck Crossing with a Minehead-bound train on 13 June 2009. This loco has been resident on the WSR since the line's reopening in 1976 having been one of the first mainline diesels to enter preservation in 1975.

Another East Lancs Railway-based diesel hydraulic that has visited the WSR on several occasions is Hymek D7076, here working an authentic ballast train round the cliff-top curve at Doniford on 15 June 2007 bound for Bishops Lydeard.

Another shot of Hymek No. D7076, this time making a thumping accent of the 1 in 65 gradient into Washford with a Bishops Lydeard-bound train on 16 June 2007.

In the 1960s BR built the Class 14 diesel hydraulic shunters at Swindon works, but the work for which they had been designed very quickly disappeared with the Beeching cuts and as a result they were withdrawn from service at just five years old! Many entered industrial service and some subsequently preservation including Nos. D9526 and D9520, here leaving Crowcombe with a Minehead-bound train on 14 June 2009. D9526 is WSR based and D9520 is privately owned and resides at the Nene Valley Railway in Peterborough.

STEAM ENGINEMAN COURSES

The railway runs some very popular experience courses where you can pay for the privilege of driving and firing a steam locomotive on the railway. On 27 March 2008 Collett 38xx 2-8-0 No. 3850 heads a driver experience course special over the former mineral line bridge at Watchet. If you would like to try your hand at driving a steam train contact the railway at www.west-somerset-railway.co.uk/sec.html

A day of clear blue skies combines with a driver experience day hauled by WSRA-owned Pannier No. 6412, standing at Williton Station with a goods train making up a stage 2 course on 4 November 2006.

The following day Pannier No. 6412 was again in action on the driver experience course goods train and climbs Washford Bank at Horse Parks on 5 November 2006.

SMALL PRAIRIES

The Great Western's small 45xx & 55xx Prairie Tanks were regular performers on the Minehead branch in GWR and BR days and still find frequent employment hauling services on today's West Somerset Railway. In more recent years Pete Waterman's No. 5553 has been the regular performer. A view across the Doniford Brook on 17 February 2008 sees No. 5553 heading uphill towards Stogumber at Castle Hill.

The low sun backlights the exhaust from No. 5542 as it rounds Roebuck Curve on 27 March 2008 bound for Bishops Lydeard. This engine was restored for use on the WSR by its owning group 5542 Ltd but spends a lot of time away from the line working elsewhere as the peak season eight-coach trains on today's WSR are too heavy for these engines and currently work can only be found for one member of the type at any time.

Another engine associated with the preserved WSR is No. 5521 which was bought from Barry scrapyard by the West Somerset Railway Association in 1975 but subsequently sold on. The engine eventually got its turn in the restoration queue and was completed at the Flour Mill workshops in the Forest of Dean for owner Bill Parker. The newly restored Prairie, complete with smokebox mounted airpump for its following trip to Poland, leaves Stogumber on 11 March 2007. This was the engine's debut in public service at that year's Spring Gala.

Prairies Nos. 5553 & 5521 double-head the Scottish Railway Preservation Society's maroon coaching stock set past Horse Parks on the climb from Blue Anchor to Washford on 24 March 2007. The coaching stock was hired from the SRPS by the WSR to provide extra capacity for the busy gala events in both 2006 and 2007 and moved from its Boness, near Edinburgh, base as an empty stock movement over Network Rail lines – further good use of the mainline link at Norton Fitzwarren.

Another double-headed small Prairie Tank combination of Nos. 5542 and 5553 heading past Roebuck Crossing on 9 March 2008. No. 5542 displays something of a hybrid livery between GWR and BR!

Rather diffused sunlight bathes Blue Anchor as No. 5542 arrives with the Bishops Lydeard-bound train on 27 March 2008.

4160

The GWR also designed and built a number of varieties of larger Prairie Tanks, the largest class of which were the 41xx and 51xx tanks. Class member No. 4160 was restored for use on the WSR under the auspices of its owning group in the early 1990s from scrapyard condition and spent 10 years in service on the WSR in BR black and then early British Railways green before being withdrawn for its 10 yearly overhaul and subsequently returned in late BR lined green livery in 2007. On 27 March that year the loco heads past Yarde Farm with the 10.30 ex Minehead service.

No. 4160 has been very popular with the crews on the WSR over its 12 years or so of service on the line. On 9 March 2008 late afternoon sunlight picks out the engine as it heads towards Bishops Lydeard at Castle Hill, Williton.

The large Prairies were often used as pilots to heavy expresses on hilly routes and No. 4160 is performing this task piloting Castle No. 5051 Earl Bathurst past Nethercott with a rake of maroon stock in typical BR 1950s style on 16 March 2007.

The well-known photo location at Castle Hill seen from a different perspective. The sun lights the up side of trains in the morning at this location and on 8 April 2008 we see No. 4160 climbing past with the 10.30 Minehead to Bishops Lydeard service.

Large Prairie No. 4160 passing Nethercott on a clear and cold 21 March 2007 with the 10.25 Bishops Lydeard to Minehead service.

9351

The WSR bought large Prairie No. 5193 in scrap condition in the late 1990s and decided to restore it as a Mogul 2-6-0 tender engine as this was deemed more suitable to the railway's requirements. Drawings exist that show that the GWR had proposals to build a class of smaller boiler 2-6-0s but the Second World War prevented this actually happening. The WSR used these drawings as the basis for the conversion work and No. 5193 was out shopped in 2004 as small Mogul No. 9351. Here the engine puts in a good effort to lift a morning train from Bishops Lydeard to Minehead up the 1 in 80 gradient at Nethercott on 6th April 2008.

Opposite
WSR Mogul No. 9351 lays a smoke screen across the site of Leigh Bridge loop as it heads towards Bishops Lydeard on 29 March 2009.

SPRING

Possibly one of the author's best-known images. WSR Mogul No. 9351 drifting downhill towards Roebuck Crossing on 13 May 2006. This was the day the West Somerset Steam Railway Trust's 1897 GWR sleeping car, the first vehicle in the train, was publicly launched following a 25 year restoration from having been included as part of a bungalow in Stogursey near Bridgwater. The vintage cars, a 1924 MG and a 1932 Talbot, were arranged by a WSSRT member and in turn the author had them positioned alongside the line at this location to await the passage of the train to create this wonderful illusion.

Early spring is evident as popular WSR-based large Prairie No. 4160 climbs the 1 in 65 gradient of Washford Bank as it passes the hamlet of Bilbrook on 27 March 2008.

Visiting Hall class 4-6-0 No. 4936 Kinlet Hall from Tyseley, Birmingham, passing Vellow Bridges near Williton with a Bishops Lydeard-bound train on 21 March 2009.

A touch of quick driving enabled me get back in front of the train and get another shot of Hall No. 4936 Kinlet Hall as it approached Crowcombe with its early morning train to Bishops Lydeard. 21 March 2009.

A dramatic spring-showers sky towers above the Quantock Hills as BR black 2-8-0T No. 5224 passes Liddymore near Williton on 9 March 2008.

A train-in-the-landscape view of Prairie No. 5542 heading past Leigh Woods near Crowcombe on 27 March 2008.

Severn Valley-based Manor No. 7802 Bradley Manor has paid a number of visits to the WSR over the years and on a breezy 18 March 2007 the engine is seen passing Nethercott with a Spring Gala service to Minehead.

Bert Hitchin's Stanier Black 5 No. 45231 Sherwood Forester helped represent the LMS at the 2009 Spring Gala and here passes Doniford on 21 March 2009.

The spring flowers are blooming as BR Standard 4 tank No. 80136 passes Yarde Farm near Stogumber on a fine 29 April 2006.

A side-on view of BR Standard 4 tank No. 80136 passing Bicknoller with a Lydeard-bound train on 29 April 2006. This was the last year of service on the WSR for this loco which had been a very reliable performer for the WSR for the previous 7 years.

SUMMER

As spring turns into summer BR Standard 2-6-4T No. 80136 passes a bright yellow rape seed crop at Liddymore near Williton on 16 April 2007.

I personally take far fewer photographs in the summer months as the light is much more harsh, warm temperatures start to make the exhaust invisible and the countryside takes on an all-over green appearance. This is starting to become evident in this shot of large Prairie No. 4160 heading past Sampford Brett on 18 May 2008 with a Bishops Lydeard-bound train.

The warm temperatures have made the exhausts invisible as classic S&D pairing of 7F No. 88 (sadly in blue livery spoiling the 1950s look) leads Bulleid No. 34067 Tangmere through the cutting on the approach to Crowcombe with a railtour that Tangmere had worked through from London heading for Minehead on 18 July 2007.

AUTUMN

The autumn tints start to show through as Driver Ron Ireland takes GW 2-8-0 No. 3850 past Castle Hill, Williton with a Bishops Lydeard-bound train on 22 October 2009.

GW 0-6-2T No. 6695, from Swanage Railway, crossing the Mineral Line Bridge soon after leaving Watchet with a Minehead-bound train on 25 October 2009.

WSR-designed small Mogul No. 9351 getting away from Blue Anchor with a Minehead-bound service on 28 October 2007.

West Somerset-based 38xx 2-8-0 No. 3850 heading a goods at Nethercott in wonderful light on 4 October 2007.

Very nice autumnal morning light illuminates GWR 0-4-2T No. 1450 doing what it was designed for, working a two coach auto train away from Crowcombe Heathfield on 5 October 2007.

WINTER

14xx tank No. 1450 heading two auto coaches in glorious winter back lighting at Combe Florey on 29 December 2007 with a Bishops Lydeard to Williton Winter Gala service.

S&D 7F No. 88 in silhouette as it climbs away from Bishops Lydeard at Watersmeet with a Santa Special working on 11 December 2005.

West Somerset-based 38xx 2-8-0 No. 3850 rounding Roebuck Curve on a cold December afternoon with a Bishops Lydeard-bound train.
28 December 2008.

A panoramic view of the West Somerset coast and countryside, with Minehead and the Butlins camp clearly visible in the distance, as No. 5553 climbs away from Blue Anchor on 16 December 2006.

WSR Mogul No. 9351 making a storming get-away from Bishops Lydeard with a Santa Express train to Williton on the frosty and misty morning of 11 December 2005. This shot can only be effectively obtained of the first train of the day in December to get the backlighting right.

King No. 6024 King Edward I passing the site of Leigh Woods loop on 30 December 2008 with a driver experience charter working from Minehead.

BR 0-6-2T No. 6695 from the Swanage Railway visited during 2008 for some repair work at the WSRA's Williton works and subsequently took part in the Winter Gala. On 28 December 2008 it is seen rounding the cliff tops at Doniford with a Lydeard-bound train.

Opposite
As winter turns back into spring Bulleid West Country No. 34046 Braunton drifts downhill at Leigh Woods with a Minehead-bound train on 22 March 2009.

DIESELS

Home-based Class 33 No. D6566, then recently repainted into BR green livery, at Liddymore between Williton and Doniford on 15 June 2008.

Class 37 diesels are very popular with diesel enthusiasts due to their distinctive and powerful sound. Carrying BR 1980s' large logo livery is class 37 No. 37190 heading a train for Minehead past Roebuck Crossing on a cloudy 7 July 2005. The engine normally resides at the Midland Railway Centre, Butterley, Derbyshire.

In original all over green livery, South Devon Railway-based class 37 No. D6737 passes Yarde Farm bound for Bishops Lydeard on 15 June 2008.

Top & Tail class 31s working a Minehead to Bristol Temple Meads service on 28 July 2007. These were regular timetabled trains introduced by Victa Westlink Rail that summer to make best use of the newly re-signalled mainline connection at Norton Fitzwarren to the Minehead branch and hopes were high that the service would develop to become a long term regular service between West Somerset and Bristol. Sadly Victa Westlink ceased trading later that year and the service did not return in 2008. It is hoped that further initiatives of this type can be introduced in the future.

A Network Rail test train visited the line on 8 April 2008 to carry out a survey and to provide the railway company with valuable information on the condition of the track. The train was top and tailed by class 31s with No. 31601 in a rather strange pink livery leading, seen here approaching Blue Anchor.

Home-based Type 2 Class 25 No. D7523 drifting downhill at Kingswood near Stogumber with a service for Minehead on 29 April 2006.

Peak 1Co-Co1 diesel No. D61 Royal Army Ordnance Corps passing Churchlands between Crowcombe and Bishops Lydeard with a train bound for the latter on 6 May 2005. This then-mainline-registered loco was visiting for the 2005 Diesel Gala Weekend and has paid several visits to the line at the head of railtours.

DOUBLE HEADED

Severn Valley Railway-based Manor No. 7802 Bradley Manor pilots Didcot's Castle No. 5051 Earl Bathurst round the curve at Kentsford with a Minehead-bound service during the railway's Spring Gala on 24 March 2007.

Opposite

A classic Western motive power combination as Llangollen Railway-based Manor No. 7822 Foxcote Manor pilots Castle No. 5051 Earl Bathurst upgrade at Watersmeet near Bishops Lydeard with a photo charter on 13 March 2007.

Turning round gave me this view of the pair as they blast their way uphill past the gathered photographers at Eastcombe, 13 March 2007.

Thought to be a preservation first – double-headed rebuilt Bulleid West Country Pacifics, Nos. 34046 Braunton and 34028 Eddystone leave Blue Anchor on 22 March 2009.

Through the still bare winter trees come Black 5 No. 45231 and Bulleid No. 34046 Braunton as they leave Bishops Lydeard on Sunday 29 March 2009.

AN A4

The first LNER A4 Pacific to run on the WSR – Jeremy Hoskin's No. 60019 Bittern passing Eastcombe shortly after leaving Bishops Lydeard with a Minehead-bound train on 22 March 2009.

Opposite
With its chime whistle sounding for Leigh Woods Crossing A4 No. 60019 Bittern passes with a Minehead-bound train on 29 March 2009.

On 22 March 2009 visiting mainline-registered A4 Pacific No. 60019 Bittern passing Nethercott with an afternoon Minehead-bound train. The engine normally resides on the Mid Hants Railway.

TORNADO EFFECT

A locomotive portrait shot of the new-build A1 Pacific No. 60163 Tornado at Minehead on 31 May 2009. This newly-constructed locomotive was built entirely from scratch by a volunteer led group who decided back in 1990 that they wanted to build an LNER A1 Pacific to plug a gap that occurred with no members of the original class being preserved. The project took some 18 years to complete and cost in excess of £3m – but what an achievement. The engine entered service in 2008 and has become very well known following TV appearances and hauling the Royal Train among others. In June 2009 the WSR secured the engine for a 3 week visit and ran a programme of additional trains for people to travel behind the engine.

Such was the popularity of the engine that the extra trains programmed to be hauled by Tornado had to be made up to 10 coaches and were still fully booked. Here an evening staff special leaves Blue Anchor behind No. 60163 on 11 June 2009.

Opposite
The brand new and already famous A1 Pacific No. 60163 Tornado leaving Blue Anchor on a sunny 9 June 2009.

A lovely coastal view at Doniford of the new-build A1 No. 60163 Tornado rounding the curve at the top of the cliffs on 14 June 2009 with another full train for Minehead.

A considerable uplift in passenger numbers was experienced by the WSR when No. 60163 Tornado worked on the line. Here the engine crosses Kerr Moor soon after leaving Blue Anchor with a Minehead-bound train on 2 June 2009.

THROUGH TRAINS

A through excursion from the Midlands on 10 March 2007 that had been worked from Hereford by Manor No. 7802 Bradley Manor, normally Severn Valley Railway-based, was joined at Bishops Lydeard by large Prairie No. 4160 to assist with the heavy train over the WSR's steep gradients, such as here on the 1 in 80 section at Churchlands, recreating a classic Western Region scene.

Another view of the same train hauled by Nos. 4160 and 7802 Bradley Manor soon after leaving Blue Anchor on the final leg to Minehead.

King No. 6024 King Edward I working a very heavy Gloucester to Minehead railtour up the gradiant at Kentsford near Watchet on 12 March 2005. The train consisted of 12 coaches and a "dead" class 50 diesel on the rear.

A through excursion returning from Minehead to London Paddington headed by a pair of Westerns, the WSR-based D1010 Western Campaigner and mainline-registered D1015 Western Champion, makes a fine sight and stirs the memories of childhood for the author as they pass Bicknoller on 16 June 2007.

AUTO TRAINS

Perhaps the classic image of a GWR auto train – Collett 0-4-2T No. 1450 with auto trailer No. 178 standing at Crowcombe Heathfield Station on 15 March 2005. Both loco and coach are owned by GWR enthusiast Mike Little and often visit various heritage lines around the UK.

An evening shot at Minehead of Pannier No. 6412 and auto coach No. 178 just after arrival and about to be stabled for the night. 17 March 2007.

Another view of auto fitted Pannier No. 6412 hauling auto coach No. 178, this time on the approach to Stogumber on 17 March 2007.

No passengers waiting so No. 5542 propels auto coach No. 178 through Doniford Halt with a Minehead-bound service on 28 December 2003.

GOODS TRAINS

Llangollen-based large Prairie No. 5199 working downhill across Woolston Moor between Stogumber and Williton with a charter goods on 4 October 2004. The Quantock Hills form a very attractive background.

Another large Prairie-hauled goods works through Stones Wood at Roebuck near Crowcombe on 14 March 2008, this time headed by home based No. 4160 with driver Ron Ireland at the controls.

Bodmin Railway-based Prairie No. 5552 visited the WSR for the Spring 2004 Gala and took the starring role on a photo charter on 23 March 2004, here passing Leigh Woods in rather dull and stormy-looking conditions.

Perhaps an unlikely turn for record breaking GWR 4-4-0 No. 3440 City of Truro working a Minehead to Bishops Lydeard goods past Roebuck crossing during the Autumn Gala on 5 October 2007.

Pannier No. 6412 leaving Blue Anchor in wonderful warm lighting with a goods working as part of a driving and firing course on 4 November 2006.

At a location strangely known as Turks Castle, near Bicknoller, is North Norfolk Railway-based J15 0-6-0 No. 65462 heading a goods charter on 22 March 2004.

Midland 4F No. 44422 heading a short goods past Nornvis Bridge on the approach to Crowcombe Heathfield on 4 October 2007. This engine was once Somerset based working from Templecombe shed on the former Somerset & Dorset system.

Class 47 No. D1661 North Star propelling an engineers train from Bishops Lydeard to Norton Fitzwarren past Longlands Farm Bridge on 29 May 2007. The loco had only recently arrived on the WSR straight out of mainline service in a deal between its former owners and the D&EPG Ltd.

HOLIDAY TRAINS TO THE WEST

As a seaside line the WSR is ideally placed to recreate the halcyon days of the holiday express when, before foreign package holidays became affordable to the masses, thousands of holiday makers made their annual trip to the seaside by train. The theme has been re-enacted by the WSR on several occasions with great success and is always popular. Here visiting Hall No. 4936 Kinlet Hall passes Helwell Bay soon after leaving Watchet on 22 March 2009.

A classic Western Region scene is recreated by the seaside at Blue Anchor as Manor No. 7822 Foxcote Manor and Castle No. 5051 Earl Bathurst work a photo charter of maroon stock across Kerr Moor in fantastic lighting conditions on 13 March 2007.

The Great Western was not the only railway to carry holiday makers to the West: the Southern also carried thousands along its Waterloo–Salisbury–Exeter route and into Devon and Cornwall on its "Withered Arm" network of lines to places such as Bude, Ilfracombe and Padstow. On 25 March 2007 Southern Bulleid West Country No. 34007 Wadebridge passes Yarde Farm during the Holiday Trains Spring 2007 Gala.

The Great Western Society Didcot-based Castle No. 5051 Earl Bathurst passing Nethercott on the afternoon of 17 March 2007 with a Minehead-bound train.

SOMERSET & DORSET 40TH ANNIVERSARY OF CLOSURE

Undoubtedly one of the most famous cross country railways in the UK, which also carried thousands of holiday makers to the coast, was the Somerset & Dorset Joint Railway from Bath to Bournemouth with a branch to Highbridge and Burnham. The network was controversially closed down in March 1966 and the anniversary is regularly marked on the WSR. On 4 March 2006 Somerset & Dorset Prussian blue liveried 7F 2-8-0 No. 88 is passing Kentsford Crossing near Watchet with a Somerset & Dorset Railway Trust special carrying an appropriate headboard.

The WSR staged major S&D galas in both 1996 and 2006 to mark the anniversary of closure and brought in a number of visiting locos appropriate to the line. These events were born following a footplate conversation between the author (as fireman) and his driver in 1995 and the WSR's hugely successful galas have been an enthusiast's must visit event each year since. Here a classic S&D pairing of 4F No. 44422, an old S&D engine itself, and Bulleid No. 34067 Tangmere is recreated for a day's photographic charter on 20 March 2006 passing Watersmeet.

The 4F No. 44422 is seen again this time piloting S&D 7F No. 53809, which was visiting for the 2006 gala, as a classic Somerset & Dorset combination climbing hard past Nethercott during the hugely successful S&D 40th Anniversary of Closure Gala on 19 March 2006. This 7F is one of two survivors of the class (the other is of course the WSR's No. 88) preserved and this was the first time the two 7Fs (53808 & 53809) had been brought together since the 1960s and the first time two 7Fs headed a train together since 1959.

The S&D was worked by a mixture of Southern and Midland-designed locomotives over the years including LMS Black 5s. In the picture No. 45440 (45407 in disguise) is rounding the long curve at Churchlands on the 4 mile climb from Bishops Lydeard to Crowcombe on 19 March 2006.

At the same location BR Black 7F No. 53809 and Bullied Battle of Britain No. 34067 Tangmere are climbing the 1 in 80 bank also on 19 March 2006. Another classic S&D combination recreated on the WSR that month. As in the previous two images the coaching stock has been digitally altered to red/cream livery rather than the WSR's usual western region choc/cream to create a more authentic S&D appearance to the shot.

S&D 7F No. 53809 & BR Std 5 No. 73129, both normally based at the Midland Railway Centre in Derbyshire, drifting downhill from Stogumber in an all too rare bit of weak sunshine whilst hauling the SRPS maroon set towards Minehead on 26 March 2006. Note how the cold water in the locos' tenders has caused them to mist up showing the current water level in each.

The Quantock Hills form an attractive backdrop to this broadside shot of Standard class 5 No. 73129 & 9F 2-10-0 No. 92203 (together creating a 14F power classification!) climbing past Nethercott on 24 March 2006 with an afternoon train to Minehead.

Driver Humphrey Davies takes David Sheppard's BR Standard 9F No. 92203 Black Prince up the final ½ mile into Crowcombe Heathfield on 19 March 2006. The 9Fs were popular and successful performers on the S&D between 1960 and 1963.

Another BR Standard 9F, this time No. 92214, also from the Midland Railway Centre, working the annual Somerset & Dorset Trust charter train towards Bishops Lydeard at Leigh Woods Crossing on 18 September 2004.

BR Standard 4 No. 76079 (acting as S&D regular 76009) piloting Bulleid No. 34067 Tangmere past Nethercott on 19 March 2006.

WEST COUNTRYS

Bulleid West Country No. 34007 Wadebridge creates a cloud of steam as it heads a Bishops-Lydeard bound service past Sampford Brett on 23 March 2007. These original condition Bulleid Pacifics became affectionately known as Spam Cans.

The rare combination of two rebuilt Bulleid West Countrys 34046 Braunton and 34028 Eddystone catch a lovely glint as they pass Leigh Woods Crossing with the 16.05 Minehead to Bishops Lydeard on 22 March 2009.

After a 10 year long restoration from scrap condition at the WSRA's Williton works West Country No. 34046 Braunton entered service during the summer of 2008. On 21 March 2009 the engine leaves Watchet at Helwell Bay.

Opposite
In the late 1950s BR commenced a rebuilding programme, which was never completed, for the Bulleid Pacifics which when carried out drastically altered their appearance. This can be seen in this view of Southern Locomotives Limited-owned Bulleid West Country No. 34028 Eddystone, from the Swanage Railway, passing Kentsford crossing near Watchet on 21 March 2009.

PHOTO CHARTERS

Photographic charters are run for the benefit of a group of photographers who pay for the privilege of having the opportunity to photograph their chosen train formation and engine at locations of their choice throughout the day. The author runs charters under his Steam Recreations banner and on 16 March 2007 Prairie No. 4160 assists Castle No. 5051 Earl Bathurst away from Bishops Lydeard at Watersmeet with a Steam Recreations special.

The charter organiser is able to request run pasts at locations where such shots may not be possible during normal timetabled services. The same charter with large Prairie No. 4160 and Castle No. 5051 Earl Bathurst is seen working downhill at Woolston on 16 March 2007.

Manor No. 7822 Foxcote Manor and Castle No. 5051 Earl Bathurst make a rousing sight and sound as they storm up the gradient at Kentsford near Watchet on 13 March 2007.

Opposite
Another classic Western Region pairing of Manor No. 7822 Foxcote Manor and Castle No. 5051 Earl Bathurst and another downhill location sees a recreation of a classic South Devon Banks mainline scene as they work round the reverse curves at Bicknoller on 13 March 2007.

Llangollen-based large Prairie No. 5199 visited the line for the 2004 Autumn Gala and is seen climbing past Nethercott in lovely late afternoon sunshine with a charter goods on 4 October 2004.

Bodmin Railway-based small Prairie No. 5552 working a photo charter runpast downhill at Nethercott on 23 March 2004.

North Norfolk Railway J15 0-6-0 No. 65462 passing Castle Hill with charter goods on 22 March 2004. The little loco visited the WSR for the Spring 2004 Gala, but it was of limited use however as its low power output meant it could not handle most WSR trains on the steep gradients.

INTO THE GLINT

North Norfolk Railway J15 0-6-0 No. 65462 picks up the late afternoon light as it rounds Roebuck Curve with a photo charter on 22 March 2004.

Pete Waterman's Prairie Tank No. 5553 passes a DMU in a typical 1960s' changeover period recreation as it approaches Bishops Lydeard early on the morning of 2 January 2004.

We close with this shot of Manor No. 7822 Foxcote Manor and Castle No. 5051 Earl Bathurst catching a strong glint from the setting sun as they cross Kerr Moor near Blue Anchor on 13 March 2007.